JULIE
THE JELLYFISH AND FRIENDS
BY J T SCOTT

JULIE
THE JELLYFISH AND FRIENDS
BY J T SCOTT

It was a quiet day at the seaside.

Julie the Jellyfish

was looking for something exciting to do.

"I wish there was something exciting to do today," said Julie.

"Maybe I'll find something exciting

in my treasure chest."

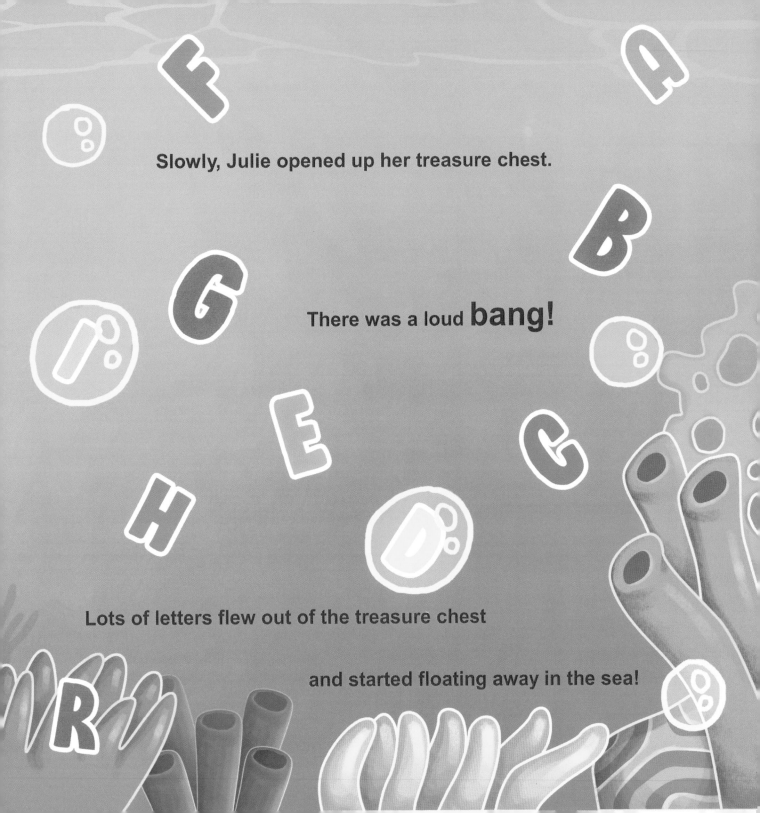

Slowly, Julie opened up her treasure chest.

There was a loud **bang!**

Lots of letters flew out of the treasure chest

and started floating away in the sea!

"Oh no!" said Julie the Jellyfish.

"All the letters are floating away!

That will keep me busy getting them all back today."

"While I swim around the sea

will you learn the letters

and sing along with me?"

Ants ate all the apples.

Bb

Bat with a bat and a ball.

Cat in a cap and a cow in a cab.

Dog and a duck dig deep in dirt.

Excited elf eats an Easter egg.

Ff

Fox finds figs with a frog in the fog.

Gg

Ghost and a ghoul play a game of golf.

Hh

Hare with a hairbrush hops in hay.

Ice-skating imp eating ice-cream.

Jewels in a jam jar in a jug.

Kid in a kilt kept a key in a kettle.

Laughing llamas love lots of limes.

Mm

Mice mix mud in a mug on the moon.

Nine nuts in a net.

Oo

Owl and an octopus open orange oats.

Pin, a peg and a pie in a pan.

Qq

Queen on a **quick** **quad** on a **quest**.

Ram on a red rug runs round rocks.

Seahorse saw a see-saw
by the sea shore.

Ten tins of tea, two teapots
and twenty teacups.

Uu

Unicorns under umbrellas.

Vv

Vet put veg in a vat by a van.

Ww

Wise whales wash with warm water.

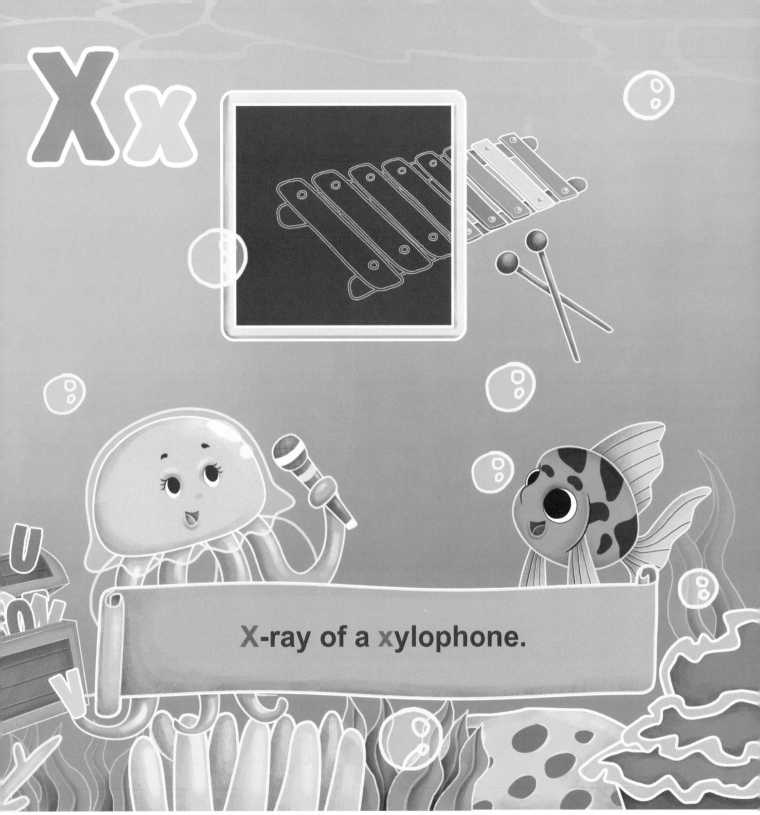

X-ray of a xylophone.

Yak ate **yoghurt** in a **yellow yacht**.

Zebra zig-zags at the zoo.

Ants ate all the apples.

Bat with a bat and a ball.

Cat in a cap and a cow in a cab.

Dog and a duck dig deep in dirt.

Excited elf eats an Easter egg.

Fox finds figs with a frog in the fog.

Ghost and a ghoul play a game of golf.

Hare with a hairbrush hops in hay.

Ice-skating imp eating ice-cream.

Jewels in a jam jar in a jug.

Kid in a kilt kept a key in a kettle.

Laughing llamas love lots of limes.

Mice mix mud in a mug on the moon.

Nine nuts in a net.

Owl and an octopus open orange oats.

Pin, a peg and a pie in a pan.

Queen on a quick quad on a quest.

Ram on a red rug runs round rocks.

Seahorse saw a see-saw by the sea shore.

Ten tins of tea, two teapots and twenty teacups.

Unicorns under umbrellas.

Vet put veg in a vat by a van.

Wise whales wash with warm water.

X-ray of a xylophone.

Yak ate yoghurt in a yellow yacht.

Zebra zig-zags at the zoo.

"Thank you everyone for joining me on my journey today,"

said Julie the Jellyfish.

"We learnt how to say the letters of the alphabet.

Let's do it again tomorrow!"

Aa Bb Cc Dd Ee
Ff Gg Hh Ii Jj
Kk Ll Mm Nn Oo
Pp Qq Rr Ss Tt
Uu Vv Ww Xx Yy Zz

JULIE
THE JELLYFISH AND FRIENDS
BY J T SCOTT

Julie the Jellyfish and Friends is dedicated to Mum & D2.

The moral right of J T Scott to be identified as the author
of this work has been asserted in accordance with the
Copyright, Designs and Patents Act 1988.

Are you ready for the next adventure?

www.bumperandfriends.com

J T SCOTT

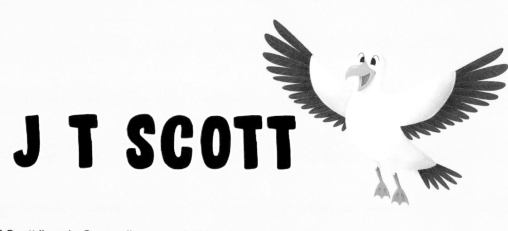

J T Scott lives in Cornwall surrounded by open countryside,

lots of castles, pens, paper and a vivid imagination.

She has also written the Sammy Rambles series

and created the inclusive game Dragonball Sport.

Sammy Rambles and the Floating Circus

Sammy Rambles and the Land of the Pharaohs

Sammy Rambles and the Angel of 'El Horidore

Sammy Rambles and the Fires of Karmandor

Sammy Rambles and the Knights of the Stone Cross

www.sammyrambles.com

www.dragonball.uk.com

Printed in Great Britain
by Amazon

79136508R00022